THE ROYAL NAVY IN SOUTH AFRICA
1900 ~ 2000

by Bill Rice

HMY Britannia alongside the Bullnose during the Royal visit in 1995.

(R Adm (JG) A.E. Rudman)

Author's Note

Although this book initially set out to be a pictorial history of the Royal Navy in Simon's Town during the twentieth century, photographs of ships in coastal waters and other South African ports have been included to provide a comprehensive picture of RN activities around the coast of South Africa. Simon's Town is no longer an RN base but strong links between the British and South African Navies remain. As I compose this note, *Glasgow* and *Black Rover* are alongside in the outer basin and St George's Street is alive with British matelots taking full advantage of the Rand/Pound exchange rate which is very much in their favour.

The compilation of this book was made possible by a number of people who, over a period of a hundred years, were sufficiently interested in their surroundings to record images of them on sensitised glass plates or film.

I owe a debt of gratitude to friends who have loaned photographs, particularly Cherry Dilley, Curator of Simon's Town Museum, Commander Mac Bisset, Director of S A Naval Museums, and Commander Chris Rawsthorne, Officer Commanding the S A Naval Printing Unit.

The task of providing suitable captions was facilitated by local residents and, in particular, the Staff and Volunteer Helpers of Simon's Town Museum and members of the Simon's Town Historical Society who have recorded the comings and goings of ships and highlights of deployments in a card index system and, in more detail, in numerous articles published in the Society Bulletin.

Allan du Toit's History of the South African Navy was consulted frequently and a sheaf of letters from Miss Calitz at the S A Naval Reference Library bears witness to the length of time the works of J.J. Colledge spent on my desk rather than on her shelves.

I am grateful to my wife and family who have supported and encouraged me during this fascinating but time consuming project and to Mike Critchley and Steve Bush at Maritime Books, in Liskeard, for their help and advice in bringing it to fruition.

First published in the United Kingdom in 2001 by Maritime Books, Lodge Hill, Liskeard, Cornwall, PL14 4EL

Printed and bound in the United Kingdom by J.H. Haynes & Co. Ltd., Sparkford. Haynes & Co. Ltd., Sparkford

The Royal Navy in South Africa 1900 - 2000

A couple of years ago Commander "Spud" Keane-Murphy, from Durban, was entertaining a group of United States Coastguardsmen in the bar of the Seven Seas Club in Simon's Town. "Spud" was waxing lyrical about Simon's Town's long and strong historic links with the "Royal Navy" when he was interrupted by one of the young Strike Craft commanders, Rory Boardman if I remember correctly, who wanted to know "Which Royal Navy? Swedish? Dutch? Danish? British?"

Considering Simon's Town's long and varied history it was a valid question so lest there be any doubt, this book is about the Royal Navy which served their Britannic Majesties Victoria, Edward VII, George V, George VI and Elizabeth II during the Twentieth Century.

Before beginning the story proper, mention should be made of two notables, now permanently resident in the Old Burial Ground at Seaforth who did not live to see the new Century. First of all William Froude, a leading engineer and hydrodynamicist of his Century, who developed the process by which the resistance of a ship could be predicted by towing a scale model through calm water. Froude contracted dysentery during a visit to Simon's Town and died at Admiralty House on 4 May 1897. He was laid to rest by the officers of the Naval vessels stationed at Simon's Town in recognition of his services to the Royal Navy. Secondly, Able Seaman Hall missed the Century by just a few months to become the first British "casualty" of the Second Anglo Boer War. Shortly after his ship, *Powerful*, arrived in Simon's Bay in 1899 to play its part in the conflict, poor old Hall suffered a fatal heart attack.

Simon's Town in 1900 was an isolated fishing and whaling community with a naval dockyard of limited resources which had been established in 1884. Private Edgar Wallace, who arrived in the Town in 1896 to take up his duties as medical orderly at the Military Hospital above the Town, considered it to be "...unexciting, little more than a ramshackle single street running haphazard along the curving spit of land which forms False Bay into a natural harbour ...." The Guardship was the Iron Turret Ship *Monarch*, launched in 1868, which was a contemporary of the ill fated *Captain*, designed by Captain Cowper Coles. The former guardship, the Screw Corvette *Penelope*, remained in the Bay as a hulk and was being used as a floating prison for Boer Prisoners of War awaiting shipment to Bermuda, Saint Helena and Ceylon (Sri Lanka).

The Flagship was the Cruiser *Doris*, supported by obsolescent Steam Gunboats and Torpedo Boats, two of which had recently been modernised and fitted with watertube boilers. The "Flat Iron Gunboats" *Griper*, *Gadfly* and *Tickler*, destined soon to be converted to Yard Craft, were still in commission and inspired Rudyard Kipling to

write the short story "Judson and the Empire" following a visit to the Town and a couple of noggins at the Officers' Club with his friend Captain Bayly.

The Dockyard had three slipways, the main one of which could take Screw Gunboats and small merchant vessels while the other two were reserved for Torpedo Boats and small craft. The Guardship and Cruisers on Station were sent round to the Robinson Graving Dock in Cape Town when underwater work was required.

Work was about to start on a new dockyard, just across Simon's Bay, with a basin and drydock which would accommodate the largest naval vessels afloat. The basin was to have a system of capstans and sheaves which would allow ships to be berthed and moved around the basin and into and out of the drydock without the aid of tugs.

Construction of the new Dockyard created a need for a variety of lighters and barges and several were sent out from the United Kingdom as crated "plates and angles" to be erected on the West Yard slipways or on the beach. One of these, the *Mooring Lighter*, formerly *Admiralty Yard Craft 221*, is still in service (2000).

In the early years of the Century, Britain was one of the major builders of warships and several called in for coal on their delivery voyages. Examples of such visits during 1913 were the Australian Battlecruiser *HMAS Australia*, escorted by the new Cruiser *HMAS Sydney*, and the Japanese Battlecruiser *HIJMS Kongo*.

Many warships were still coal fired and the new yard had coaling sheds along the East Wall which were capable of storing 10,000 tons. These were kept filled with good "Welsh Cobbles" by a fleet of colliers, most of which came and went without incident. Exceptions were the Turret Steamer *SS Clan Stuart*, which ran aground at Glencairn in 1914 (the cylinder block of her triple expansion steam engine can still be seen projecting above water just offshore) and the *SS Lundy Light*, which managed to ram the breakwater on the way in to harbour in July 1928 and spent three weeks in the graving dock having her bows rebuilt.

The outbreak of World War I highlighted the strategic importance of the base at Simon's Town and the local squadron was increased in strength after the battle of Coronel, although the ships were later withdrawn after the British victory at the Falklands. The Cape squadron was later augmented by the Japanese cruisers *HIJM Ships Niitaka* and *Tsushima*, which remained on station until the end of the War.

The "Twenties" saw the arrival of three ex Royal Naval vessels to form the South African Naval Service and also the old cruiser *Thames*, which became the S A Training Ship *General Botha*. The departure of *Lowestoft* from the station in 1928 signalled a reduction in the requirement for coal to be stored for bunkering naval vessels and the subsequent need for a bunker oil storage facility. World War I had shown the need for a powerful seagoing tug at Simon's Town and the **Saint Dogmael**, built in Hong Kong during the War, arrived to spend most of her life there. She was joined for a short while by **Saint Bees** and **Saint Aubin**.

The early 1930's were lean years which saw, among other things, the disbanding of the fledgling S A Naval Service. Towards the end of the decade the modern cruisers **Amphion** and **Neptune** were on station and men of the RNVR (SA) received sea training in the run-up to the inevitable war.

World War II was a busy time for the Navy and the Dockyard. Additional accommodation was required for accompanied RN personnel and "Home Agreement" Dockyardmen and their families. During 1943 two blocks of flats, named Hamoaze Court and Solent Court were built on Runciman Drive, overlooking the town, together with a group of officers' houses named Medway Terrace, just across the road.

The biggest job undertaken during the war was the rebuilding of the fore end of the Aircraft Carrier **Hermes**, following her collision with the **AMC Corfu**.

During the War the sides of the Graving Dock were decorated with the badges of visiting ships. Resplendent among them is the badge of the American Cruiser **USS Marblehead** which, badly damaged by Japanese bombers, limped into Simon's Town unannounced in 1942, having been reported sunk in the Java Sea. Three weeks later she had been repaired sufficiently to allow her to sail for the U.S.A.

Sailors ashore during the War were able to relax in a number of clubs, pubs and hotels in the village. Those wishing to venture farther afield could take the train to Cape Town. The distance from "Snoekie" to the "Mother City" was twenty two miles and anybody dying of thirst on the way could hop off for a "wet" at one of the twenty two railway stations on the way and continue his journey later. One of the popular haunts was the "Spotty Dog" Cafe at Lakeside, which had a large effigy of a sitting dalmation outside. As well as being popular with RN sailors, "Spotty Dog" is reputed to have been frequented by Nazi agents and sympathisers, eager to obtain information on ship movements. The site of "Spotty's" is marked today by a small replica of the original "dog."

One of the Simon's Town "characters" of the War was the great dane "Able Seaman Just Nuisance" who commuted by train between Simon's Town and the Union Jack Club in Cape Town. "Nuisance" died at Simon's Town on 1 April 1944 and was buried, at the Signal Station on Redhill, with full military honours.

After the War, a light cruiser and two sloops were based at Simon's Town, which was a pleasant posting for R.N. personnel, free of the food shortages and rationing being experienced "back 'ome". So attractive was the Cape lifestyle that when the Survey Ship **Dalrymple** was ready to sail for the coast of East Africa on completion of her refit in 1954, one third of the ship's company was "adrift."

Joint RN/SAN exercises were held in the years following the war. Some of these involved close encounters of the unfortunate kind including **Norfolk** v **SAS Natal**, **SAS Simon van der Stel** v **Pelican**, **Diomede** v **Tidepool** and the more serious **SAS Pietermaritzberg** v **Leopard**.

A feature of the Dockyard in the late 1940's was the South Atlantic Reserve Fleet, comprising the "W" Class Destroyers **Kempenfeldt**, **Wager**, **Wessex** and **Whelp**, which lay against the East Wall. The Flotilla Leader, **Kempenfeldt**, was the living-in ship and was fairly well maintained, while the others were rather neglected. **Wessex** and **Whelp**, on board which HRH the Duke of Edinburgh had served as First Lieutenant, were later purchased by the South African Government whilst **Kempenfeldt** and **Wager** were towed back to the United Kingdom and later transferred to Yugoslavia.

The Naval Base and Dockyard were transferred to the South African Government on 1 April 1957 and the Simon's Town Agreement was signed, allowing the Royal Navy to use the base facilities and to store fuel and ammunition, in return for providing technical support and assistance with training.

Access to the facilities of the Simon's Town base became particularly important to the Royal Navy during the two periods when the Suez Canal was closed.

In the early nineteen seventies the South African Navy constructed a dedicated submarine base and Synchrolift. With the Lift in operation the West Yard slipway was decommissioned and the graving dock tended to be under utilized.

Joint exercises continued into the 1970's, when the Simon's Town Agreement was abrogated. Throughout the late '60's and early '70's, Royal Naval ships and submarines visited Simon's Town on their way to and from the Beira Patrol, which was instigated to prevent the flow of oil to Rhodesia via the pipeline from the Mozambiquan port.

The Dockyard was extensively modernized in the late nineteen seventies and an outer basin was constructed, dramatically increasing the number of ships that could be berthed.

For more than nineteen years, from the mid 1970's to the early 1990's, no RN ships visited Simon's Town although RFAs did occasionally call.

The link was restored when the Type 23 Frigate **Norfolk** visited Simon's Town on 31 January 1994. She was followed in 1995 by the Royal Yacht **Britannia**, with HM Queen Elizabeth II on board, and in 1997 by the Type 22 Frigate **Chatham**, which attended the South African Navy's 75th anniversary celebrations.

Bill Rice
Simon's Town 2001

At the end of the Nineteenth Century the naval base at Simon's Town was located on the site of the present day West Dockyard. In 1885 the Admiralty purchased the facility previously operated by the insolvent Simon's Bay Patent Slipway Company, and renamed it No. 1 Slip. Two smaller slips for torpedo boats and other small craft were later added. The photograph shows the 805 ton Gunboat (lst. Class) *Thrush*, launched by Scotts at Greenock in 1889 on No. 1 Slip. No. 2 Slip is occupied by *Torpedo Boat No.6* and No. 3 slip by *Torpedo Boats No.028* (ahead) and *No.029*. *TB No.028* was severely damaged due to stranding and was expended as a target during 1898, being replaced by *TB No.060* which arrived at the Cape on 5 January 1901. *TB No.6* was sold in April 1907 and was broken up at the Cape. In the background are (left to right) the 5600 ton cruiser *Doris*, the prison hulk *Penelope*, and the Guardship *Monarch*, launched at HM Dockyard Chatham on 25 May 1868 as an Iron Turret Ship.   (Simon's Town Museum)

Slipways, looking inland: Opposite the West Yard Gate, at the head of the slipways, was St. George's Street, at the other side of which was the British Hotel, one of several establishments frequented by matelots serving at the Cape in the early years of the Twentieth Century. The photograph shows Torpedo Boats on Slipways 2 and 3. The boat on the left is probably *Torpedo Boat No. 6*, built by J.I.Thornycroft in 1878, which was later broken up at the Cape. (Africana Museum, Johannesburg).

Until the Selborne Graving Dock was opened in 1910 the larger ships based at Simon's Town or visiting the Cape had to go to Cape Town when drydocking was required. This photograph shows *Monarch*, in the Robinson Dock at Cape Town in 1898. *Monarch*, launched at Chatham in 25 May 1868, embodied the Admiralty designers' ideas concerning the freeboard required by a Turret Ship in order to ensure adequate stability. These ideas were opposed by Captain Cowper Coles, who gained sufficient support to have *Captain*, a low freeboard Turret Ship, built by Laird at Birkenhead, in 1869. *Captain* capsized in the Bay of Biscay on 7 September 1870 in a storm which *Monarch* survived, vindicating the opinions of the Chief Constructor, Edward J.Reed. *Monarch* was the Guardship at the Cape from 1897 to 1904, when she became a Depot Ship and was renamed *Simoom*. In 1905 she left Simon's Town, under her own steam, to be broken up in England.

(Cape Archives)

Early in the Twentieth Century, Simon's Town was still a very minor base with a camber providing shelter for small boats and with three slipways which could be used to haul out torpedo boats, gunboats and yard craft. This view of Simon's Bay, looking from the bridle path on Redhill, shows, from the left (West) side - the Mooring Vessel *Swift* (built at Deptford in 1835 as a packet brig) the Cruisers *Fox* and *Doris* with the Guardship *Monarch* behind. Further to the right (East) is a Barracouta Class Cruiser with the hulk *Penelope* behind. Between the two Thrush class Steam Gunboats are the "Flat Iron Gunboats" *Griper*, *Gadfly* and *Tickler*. In front of the group is a Torpedo Boat, possibly *No. 6*.

(Simon's Town Museum)

HMS Rambler, pictured here with the Flagship *Doris*, was launched as a Composite Screw Gunvessel from John Elder's Fairfield Yard at Govan on 26 January 1880, but was converted to a Survey Vessel four years later. She was based in Simon's Town during the Second Anglo Boer War (1899 - 1902) and was sold out of the Service on 23 January 1907.

(Simon's Town Museum)

The Eclipse Class Protected Cruiser **Doris**, launched at Barrow-in-Furness on 3 March 1896, landed 4.7" guns to support British troops during the Second Anglo-Boer War. The guns were mounted on carriages designed by Captain Percy Scott and manufactured, in a very short time, by the artisans of Simon's Town Dockyard. Four 4.7" guns and four twelve pounders, taken from **Doris** and **Barrosa**, were manned by the Naval Brigade at the Battle of Modder River on 3 February 1900. Captain Scott, who commanded **Terrible** during the Anglo-Boer War, was to play a leading part in the naval gunnery revolution of the early 1900s.

(Simon's Town Museum)

HM Torpedo Boat No.029 belonged to a group of fifty seven First Class Torpedo Boats built by J.l.Thornycroft between 1885 and 1886. Similar boats with slightly different dimensions and speeds were built by Yarrow and J. Samuel White. When World War I broke out, the Cape Squadron was away on its annual East Coast Cruise, leaving only *TB No.029* and her sister *No.060*, to defend Simon's Town against any seaborne attack. Despite their obsolescence, one of the Boats captured the German *SS Rufidji* off Cape Point on 18 August 1914 and brought her into Simon's Town as a prize.

(Simon's Town Museum)

The eighth **St. George** in the Royal Navy was a cruiser of the Edgar class, launched by Earle of Hull, on 23 June 1892. In 1895 she became the flagship of Rear Admiral Sir Harry Rawson, at Simon's Town. During August of the following year she was involved in resolving a succession crisis resulting from the death of the Sultan of Zanzibar. Following an ultimatum issued by the C-in-C, the cruiser *Philomel* and the gunboat *Thrush* bombarded the palace and the usurper surrendered. From March to October 1901, **HMS St George** formed part of the escort for the Orient liner *Ophir*, which had been chartered by the Duke and Duchess of Cornwall and York, later to be King George V and Queen Mary, on a World cruise. During 1908/9 she was converted to a Destroyer Depot Ship and served as such during World War 1. She was sold for scrap at Plymouth on 1 July 1920. (Simon's Town Museum)

The fifth **Beagle** was a Sloop of 1170 tons displacement, mounting eight five-inch guns. She was launched at HM Dockyard Portsmouth on 28 February 1889 and was stationed at the Cape from 9 September 1901 until 29 September 1903. She is believed to have been the last vessel on the Station to use sails. She was sold out of the Service on 11 July 1905.

(Simon's Town Museum)

At the turn of the Century, with work starting on the new dockyard, a requirement arose for steel lighters and other Yard Craft. These were often prefabricated in British shipyards and sent out in crates to be reassembled in Simon's Town. This photograph, taken on a misty Glasgow morning, shows a hopper barge being assembled, using bolts instead of rivets, prior to being shipped out to the Cape. The hopper barge was eventually assembled on the beach at Simon's Town by Messrs Perrott, and was launched on 17 October 1902.

(SA Naval Museum)

The Edgar class Protected Cruiser **Gibraltar**, launched on the Clyde on 27 April 1892, was the flagship of Sir Arthur W. Moore at Simon's Town. She is seen here dressed overall in 1902, presumably celebrating either the Coronation of King Edward VII or the end of the Anglo-Boer War. **Gibraltar** served during World War 1, initially at the Anti-Submarine School at Portland and later as a depot ship. She was sold to John Cashmore in September 1923 and broken up at Newport, Monmouthshire.

(Simon's Town Museum)

This photograph, taken from above the Town on 26 December 1903, gives an impression of the number and variety of vessels based at or visiting Simon's Bay in the early years of the Twentieth Century. In the background the new East Dockyard can be seen taking shape and, in the middle distance, the array of tugs, lighters and specialist craft associated with the construction project. Naval vessels in the bay are, from left to right - the Flagship *Gibraltar*, the 3rd class cruisers *Barrosa* and *Barracouta*, the Guardship *Monarch* and the 2nd Class cruiser *Forte*. In the background are the steam colliers *Terra* and *Berea*, keeping the fleet supplied with good hard "Welsh Cobbles," which were found to be far better for producing steam than the softer South African coal. Finally, in the foreground is the steam yacht *Nerissa*, of the Royal Yacht Squadron.   (Cape Archives)

The construction of a dockyard, complete with a sheltered basin and dry-dock large enough to accommodate Battleships and Battle Cruisers and a comprehensive set of shipyard workshops, transformed Simon's Town from a small fishing village to a bustling Dockyard Town. It was soon able to cater for all the requirements of the ships and the officers and men who served in them. The work was undertaken by Sir John Jackson, who brought in skilled workers from several countries to build and fit out the facility. "Jackson's Quarry," from which stone blocks were sent down for the construction of the dry-dock and dockyard buildings, still scars the mountainside above the yard. This photograph, taken on 6 January 1906, shows the Selborne Graving Dock being constructed within a cofferdam. The coaling sheds along the East Wall can also be clearly seen.

(Simon's Town Museum)

The Protected Cruiser *Edgar*, name ship of her class, was launched at Devonport Dockyard on 24 November 1890. Together with her sisters *Endymion*, *Theseus* and *Grafton*, she was rebuilt in 1914/15 with anti-torpedo bulges and nets for service in the Dardanelles. She survived World War 1 and was sold on 9 May 1921, arriving at Morecambe on 3 April 1923.

(Simon's Town Museum)

HMS Edgar arrived in Simon's Bay on 29 September 1908 flying the flag of Rear Admiral G. Le C. Egerton CB, manned by the relief crew for *HMS Hermes*. She secured to No.2 buoy and the flag was transferred to *Hermione*. On 3 October *Hermes* (on the left) and *Edgar* exchanged ships' companies and *HMS Edgar* sailed for England on 6 October - the date on which this photograph was taken.

(Simon's Town Museum)

The 1,070 tons Sloop **Odin**, armed with six four-inch guns, was launched at Sheerness Dockyard on 30 November 1901 and arrived at Simon's Town on 16 May 1903. After carrying out East and West coast patrols she paid off on 4 November 1904 and her ship's company was transferred to the Depot Ship **Simoom**, formerly **HMS Monarch**, for passage back to Britain. She was laid up on various buoys in the Bay until December 1909 when she embarked a passage crew and loaded one hundred tons of coal from the Hulk **Nubian** (C 370). She sailed for England via Cape Town on 3 January 1910. **Odin** was one of a handful of old Sloops which were retained in service for patrol duties during World War I. She was sold at Bombay (now Mumbai) on 12 November 1920.

(Simon's Town Museum)

Terra Nova arrived at Simon's Town on 15 August 1910, under the command of Lieutenant E.R.G.R. Evans RN (who was destined to return some years later as C-in-C having gained fame during World War I as "Evans of the *Broke*.") The ship was joined at Simon's Town by Captain Robert Falcon Scott RN, who had been on a fundraising tour of South Africa, before sailing for New Zealand en route to Antarctica. She flew the White Ensign as an honorary member of the Royal Yacht Squadron.   (Simon's Town Museum)

The Selborne Graving Dock, with a length on the blocks of 750 feet and entrance width of 95 feet, was officially opened by HRH the Duke of Connaught on 3 November 1910. It was named in honour of the Earl of Selborne GCMG, High Commissioner to South Africa, who laid the foundation stone on 15 November 1906. Following the opening ceremony, the Survey Vessel *Mutine* became the first commissioned vessel to be dry-docked. The 980 ton vessel was launched by Lairds of Birkenhead on 1 March 1900 and was converted for survey duties seven years later. She survived World War I to become an RNVR Drill Ship in 1925 and was later sold on 16 August 1932 to be broken up by T.W. Ward at Briton Ferry. (Simon's Town Museum)

The Flagship of the Cape Station, **Hermes** was the second vessel to make use of the Selbourne Graving Dock, docking down on 10 November 1910, the day after **Mutine** had vacated it. On her return to the United Kingdom, **Hermes** underwent conversion to become the Royal Navy's first aircraft carrier. She commissioned in May 1913 with a tracked "take-off platform" over the forecastle for launching a Caudron amphibian but later carried three Short "Folder" seaplanes which were launched and recovered using a crane. She was torpedoed and sunk by **U-27** in the Straits of Dover on 31 October 1914.

(SA Naval Museum)

Simon's Bay in 1911: The ships shown here are, from left to right, the Cruiser *Forte*, the Hulk *Penelope*, the Survey Vessel *Mutine*, the 3rd Class Cruiser *Pandora*, the 2nd Class Cruiser *Glasgow* and the 340 tons Water Boat *Chub*. *Glasgow* was dry-docked on 2 November 1911 and undocked on 18 November. On 11 July 1882 *Penelope*, together with *Monarch*, gained the battle honour "Alexandria" while bombarding the fortress during the Egyptian Crisis preceding the British victory at Tel-el-Kebir. The Armoured Corvette *Penelope* was the first British warship to have dedicated washing facilities for all members of the ship's company.

(Simon's Town Museum)

The Second Class Cruiser *Forte*, 4,360 tons, launched at Chatham Dockyard on 9 December 1893, arrived at Simon's Town in 1909 and remained on station until 1913. On 1 August 1909 she sailed for the Eastern Cape to search for Lund's Blue Anchor Line steamer *Waratah*, which was overdue on a voyage from Australia via Durban. She was joined by *Pandora* and the Flagship, *Hermes* but, as is well known, found no trace of the ill fated ship. On 30 November 1909 she was placed in the Selborne Graving Dock afloat to have a condemned gun mounting removed and replaced. Although she did not dock down she was, technically, the first commissioned ship to make use of the new Graving Dock. On 18 April 1911, at around midnight, the Portugese liner *Lusitania*, with almost 800 people onboard, ran onto Bellows Rock, just off Cape Point, and began to sink. The tug *Scotsman* was sent from Simon's Town at around 02:00 to assist and *Forte* was ordered to raise steam and join her as soon as possible. The sea was calm and *Scotsman* took off approximately 400 people and returned to Simon's Town while *Forte* rescued the remainder and landed them at Cape Town. *Forte* missed service in the First World War, being sold on 2 April 1914 to Dutch shipbreakers. (Cape Archives)

25

The Pelorus Class Protected Cruiser *Pandora*, launched at Portsmouth Dockyard on 17 January 1900, was one of the ships involved in the search for the Liner *Waratah* in 1909 (see previous page). She was sold on 7 October 1913 to T.W. Ward to be broken up at Morecambe. It is interesting to compare the docking practise, shown here, of using a large number of breastshores, with the modern practise of providing bottom and bilge supports with few, if any breastshores.

(SA Naval Museum)

The 4,470 tons Armoured Corvette *Penelope*, launched at Pembroke Dockyard on 18 June 1867, took part in the bombardment of Alexandria on 11 July 1882. In 1891 she was sent to the Cape to serve as Guardship at Simon's Town, being replaced by the Iron Turret Ship *Monarch* in 1897, after which she was reduced to a hulk. During the Second Anglo-Boer War she was used as a floating prison for Boer Prisoners awaiting shipment to Saint Helena, Bermuda and Ceylon (Sri Lanka). The three masted hulk, *Penelope*, shown in the basin at Simon's Town with *Hyacynth*, was sold on 12 July 1912 and was towed to Genoa where she was broken up.

(Cape Archives)

The 21,300 ton Battlecruiser *HMAS Australia*, Flagship of the Royal Australian Navy, was launched by John Brown & Co. Ltd at Clydebank on 25 October 1911 and completed on 21 June 1913. She sailed for Australia soon afterwards in company with *HMAS Sydney*, calling at Simon's Town on the way. During World War I she initially served in Australian waters but sailed for England in December 1914. She sank the German merchant vessel *S S Elenore Woermann* off the Falklands and served as Flagship of the Second Battlecruiser Squadron, colliding with the Battlecruisers *New Zealand* and *Repulse* before returning to Australia in 1919. She paid off on 12 December 1921 and was scuttled off Sydney (to satisfy the requirements of the Washington Treaty) on 12 April 1924.

(Simon's Town Museum)

The Japanese Battlecruiser *HIJMS Kongo*, built by Vickers Armstrong in 1913, called at Simon's Town on her delivery voyage to Japan and anchored in the Bay close to *Hyacinth*. The tug in the foreground of the photograph is *Scotsman*, which was involved in the rescue of passengers and crew from the Portuguese liner *Lusitania* in 1911. The Battlecruiser *Tiger*, arguably one of the best looking capital ships ever built, was originally to have been completed as a unit of the Lion Class but was modified to incorporate some of the design features of *Kongo*. During World War 1 Japan and Great Britain were allies and the two Japanese Cruisers were thus based at Simon's Town.

(Cape Archives)

The Battle Cruiser *Indefatigable*, which blew up and sank at the Battle of Jutland, had two sisters, **HMAS *Australia*** and **HMS *New Zealand***, both of which visited Simon's Town in 1913. The construction of ***New Zealand*** (seen here) was funded by the people of the country after which she was named, was launched by the Fairfield Shipbuilding and Engineering Co. Ltd, at Govan, on 1 July 1911. She was completed in December 1912 and visited Simon's Town and Cape Town in March of the following year. During World War I she took part in the Battles of Heligoland Bight, Dogger Bank and Jutland. In 1919 she was sent on a tour of "The Dominions," calling at Simon's Town and Cape Town. One of the ships listed for disposal under the Washington Treaty she was sold on 10 December 1922 and later broken up at Rosyth.

(Simon's Town Museum)

The Light Cruiser **HMAS Sydney** was one of three Australian Cruisers whose design was based on the Chatham Class. She was completed by the London & Glasgow Shipbuilding Co. Ltd. (later Harland & Wolff Ltd., Govan) in June 1913 and arrived in Simon's Town on 26 August, escorting the Battle Cruiser **HMAS Australia**. Both ships entered the basin on arrival and remained alongside the coaling berths until 28 August when they anchored out in the bay, continuing their journey to Australia the following day. On 9 November 1914, **HMAS Sydney** sank the German Raider **Emden** at Cocos Keeling Island. She was broken up in 1928 and in 1934 her tripod foremast was erected at Bradley's Head, in Sydney Harbour, to commemorate her victory. It can still be seen there today (2000).

(Simon's Town Museum)

31

The German steamer **Rufidji** owned by the Deutsch Ost-Afrika Line, was intercepted off Cape Point on 18 August 1914 by one of the Torpedo Boats based at Simon's Town and escorted into Simon's Bay. In keeping with the practice of giving captured German merchant vessels names beginning with the prefix "Hun," **Rufidji** was renamed **Huntscliff**. She was allocated to the Union Castle Line and almost survived the War, but was sunk in the Atlantic in October 1918.

(Simon's Town Museum)

The Augmented Cape of Good Hope Squadron, December 1914: At the outbreak of World War I, the C-in-C, Rear Admiral H.G. King Hall, had the Cruisers *Hyacinth* (Flagship), *Astraea* and *Pegasus* at his disposal. Following the Battle of Coronel, which left the German China Squadron free to roam the Southern Oceans, the Cape of Good Hope Squadron was strengthened by the arrival of the pre-Dreadnought battleship *Albion*, the Armoured Cruisers *Minotaur* and *Defence* and the Light Cruisers *Weymouth* and *Dartmouth*. Following the British victory at the Battle of the Falklands, these ships were withdrawn and the squadron was reinforced by the Cruisers *Challenger*, *Talbot* and *Minerva*, the sloops *Thistle* and *Rinaldo* and eleven Armed Whalecatchers. In this photograph, taken in December 1914, are, from left to right :

Outer row: *S S Clan Stuart* (grounded and wrecked at Glencairn on 20 November 1914), *RMS Armadale Castle* and two colliers. Middle row: *HM Ships Dartmouth* and *Minotaur* and the SAR & H tug *Ludwig Weiner* (later *HMS Afrikander*). Nearest row: *HM Ships Weymouth*, *Astraea* and *Albion*.   (Simon's Town Museum)

The 10,412 grt P&O liner *Macedonia* was taken over by the Admiralty on 2 August 1914 and was returned to her owners in November 1918. At the Battle of the Falkland Islands in December 1914 **AMC** *Macedonia*, in company with the cruiser *Bristol*, was involved in sinking the German Cruiser **SMS** *Baden* and the transport *Santa Isabel*. During 1917, while based at Simon's Town, she went to the aid of the Blue Funnel Line cargo liner *Tyndareus*, which had struck a mine laid by the German Raider *Wolf*, and towed her stern first to Simon's Town. *Tyndareus* was badly damaged forward but was repaired in the graving dock between 12 February and 25 May 1917.

(Simon's Town Museum)

The Bristol Class cruiser *Glasgow* called at Simon's Town during 1915, following her participation in the battles of Coronel and the Falklands. The censor's stamp on the back of the photograph bears the date 24 April 1915. *Glasgow*, a product of the Fairfield shipyard at Govan, went on to serve with the 8th Light Criuser Squadron in the Mediterranean before being sold on 29 April 1927 to T.W. Ward & Co, to be broken up at Morecambe.
(Simon's Town Museum)

The Pre-Dreadnought Battleship *Vengeance*, of the Canopus Class, was launched at Barrow-in-Furness on 25 July 1899. During World War I she operated in Cameroon (1914), the Dardanelles, East Africa and the East Indies (1915). After the war she was used as a Depot Ship until she was sold in December 1921, to be broken up at Dover.   (Simon's Town Museum)

The 15,495 ton *Orbita* was launched at Belfast in July 1914 as a passenger and cargo liner for the Pacific Steam Navigation Co. Ltd. but was completed during the following year as an AMC. She was based at Simon's Town until being transferred to the Falkland Islands in February 1916. Later in the War she served as a troopship before being returned to her owners, sailing on her maiden voyage from Liverpool to Valparaiso via the Panama Canal in Septermber 1919. *Orbita* was used as a troopship during World War II and in 1946 was chartered by the Ministry of Transport as an emigrant ship. She was eventually broken at Newport, Monmouthshire, in 1950.

(Simon's Town Museum)

During 1899, two non propelled mooring lighters were ordered by the British Admiralty from Messrs. Fleming and Ferguson of Paisley, Scotland. *Lighter No. 30* (Yard No. 286) was launched on 15 March 1900 for service at HM Dockyard Sheerness and components for *Lighter No. 14* (Yard No. 285) were marked and crated for shipment to the Cape of Good Hope Yard at Simon's Town. Payment for the two lighters was to be subject to successful completion of acceptance trials of *Lighter No. 30*. *Lighter No. 14* was assembled on No. 1 slipway in the West Dockyard at Simon's Town and was first launched on 17 October 1901. The boiler was lifted on board and she was hauled back up on the slip later in the day to be completed, being launched for service on 19 February 1902. Following several rebuilds and replacement of the steam plant with a diesel/hydraulic system the vessel, once known as *Yard Craft 221* but now just *"The Mooring Lighter"* is still in service (2000), doing the job for which she was designed more than a century earlier.

(Simon's Town Museum)

The minesweeper *Ventnor*, ordered from Wm. Simons Ltd of Renfrew and launched on 1 July 1919 as *Verwood*, was one of six Aberdare Class ships selected for conversion to Survey Ships and commissioned as *Crozier.* In 1921 she was handed over to the Government of the Union of South Africa and arrived at Simon's Town on 11 January 1922, being transferred to the South African Naval Service on 1 April, becoming *HMSAS Protea.* Due to cuts in defence spending she was destored and paid off, being handed back to the Royal Navy on 30 April 1933. She was sold to Protea Show Boat (Pty) Ltd for the sum of £1000 and spent some time as a rather gaudy floating nightclub and cruise ship, operating out of Cape Town. She was sold again in 1935 and was sailed back to the UK where she operated out of Blackpool as the pleasure steamer *Queen of the Bay*. Her high rate of coal consumption made her uneconomical and she was sold again. However, she was saved from the scrapyard because, with a speed of 16 knots she was an attractive proposition as a blockade runner in the Spanish Civil War, which broke out in 1936. The ship was demolished after running aground in Gibraltar Bay during 1939.   (Simon's Town Museum)

The Second Class Cruiser *Thames*, mounting two eight-inch and ten six-inch guns, was launched at Pembroke Dockyard on 3 December 1885. Outdated at the turn of the Century, she was converted to a Submarine Depot Ship and served as such during World War I. She was purchased on 13 November 1920 by Mr. T.B.F. Davis, of Durban, and was sailed to Cape Town, arriving on 26 March 1921. She was converted to a training ship for boys intending to pursue a career at sea and was moved round to Simon's Town where she was commissioned on 15 March 1922 as *SATS General Botha* in memory of the first Prime Minister of the Union of South Africa. Many of her alumni had distinguished careers, including four Chiefs of the South African Navy, but almost certainly the most famous product of the *"Bothie"* was the Battle of Britain Fighter Ace "Sailor" Malan.

(Simon's Town Museum)

The Special Service Squadron, comprising the battlecruisers *Hood* and *Repulse* and the Light Cruisers *Delhi, Dauntless, Danae, Dragon* and *Dunedin* set off from England on 27 November 1923 for a round the World Cruise, spending Christmas at the Cape. News of the Squadron's impending visit was not received by the C-in-C but by Captain Gordon Campbell V.C., in his capacity as Controlling Authority for the Base Canteen, when a requisition for a large number of turkeys, christmas puddings and crates of beer, wine and spirits arrived! During the visit *Dragon* was involved in a collision in Table Bay Docks and an emergency drydocking had to be arranged at Simon's Town in order to effect repairs to her stern. The photograph shows (from left to right) *Repulse, Lowestoft (Flagship), Birmingham*, two Arabis Class Sloops and the Salvage Tug *St Dogmael*.   (Simon's Town Museum)

The two-funneled Arabis Type Minesweeping Sloop ***Wallflower***, a variant of the Flower Class, was launched at Irvine, on the Ayrshire Coast, on 8 November 1915. She served as a minesweeper and convoy escort during World War I and remained in service until 1931, unlike most of the class which had been sold by 1923. (Simon's Town Museum)

East Dockyard 1926: This photograph shows an Arabis Type Minesweeping Sloop, possibly *Wallflower*, afloat in the graving dock with the "A" section of the dock empty and dry. The Flagship, *Birmingham*, is at the West Wall North and another Sloop is berthed on the East Wall. Just to the right of the graving dock is the circular Martello Tower, built in 1795 as a signal station and lookout point.

(Simon's Town Museum)

HMS Lowestoft, a cruiser of the Birmingham Class, was launched at Chatham Dockyard on 23 April 1913 and completed during the following year. She took part in the Battle of Heligoland Bight in 1914 and served in the Mediterranean for the remainder of the War. She arrived at the Cape in 1920 and was the Flagship of V.Adm. Sir R.W. Bentinck from 1922 to 1925. She was the last coal fired Cruiser to serve at the Cape and is seen here leaving Cape Town, with Devils' Peak in the background, in the late nineteen twenties. *Lowestoft* was sold on 8 January 1931 and broken up at Milford Haven.

(Simon's Town Museum)

The 5,440 ton Light Cruiser *Birmingham* was launched into the River Tyne on 7 May 1913. She served with the Grand Fleet in 1914 and had the distinction of claiming the first U-Boat "kill" of World War I when she sank *U-15* on 9 August 1914. *Birmingham* gained battle honours at Heligoland, Dogger Bank and Jutland. Between 1920 and 1928 she served as Flagship to three Commanders-in-Chief at the Cape. This photograph shows the ship at Mossel Bay (with either the *RMS Windsor Castle* or *RMS Arundel Castle* in the background) and was taken during her last East Coast Cruise, flying the flag of Vice Admiral D. Murray-Anderson. She left Simon's Town for Chatham on 10 August 1928 and was sold for scrap in 1931, arriving at Pembroke Dock on 12 March.

(Simon's Town Museum)

HMS Carlisle: This "C" Class Light Cruiser was launched at Govan on 9 July 1918 - too late to see service during World War I although her sister **Cardiff,** launched from the same yard three months earlier, had the honour of leading the surrendered German High Seas Fleet into Scapa Flow. She joined the Cape of Good Hope Squadron in 1928, replacing **Lowestoft,** and served on station until she herself was relieved by **Neptune** on 16 March 1937. On her return to England, **Carlisle** was placed in reserve but was later taken in hand in 1939 for conversion to an anti-aircraft cruiser. She was damaged beyond repair by an air attack in the Mediterranean on 9 October 1943 and became a depot ship, and later a hulk, at Alexandria, where she was broken up in 1948.

(Simon's Town Museum)

In 1933 Tschekedi Khama, the acting ruler of the Bechuanaland Protectorate (known today as Botswana) precipitated a crisis by ordering that a white man be flogged, after being tried in a native court. As the High Commissioner was out of the Country, his deputy, the Naval C-in-C, Vice Admiral E.R.G.R. Evans, was required to take action. Evans and his Naval and Royal Marine Escort, drawn from **Carlisle, Rochester and Weston**, left Simon's Town by train on 10 September 1933. The expedition met no resistance from local tribesmen and Evans arranged a parade of the Armed Escort at which he formally deposed Chief Tschekedi Khama, who had been ruling the Protectorate while Seretse Khama was still a minor. Subsequently the deposed chieftain asked permission to visit the C-in-C at Simon's Town, where he apologised for his actions. He was reinstated at a ceremony during which Evans read the contents of Khama's written apology, which had been drafted aboard **Dorsetshire**, to his assembled tribesmen. The photograph shows Lieutenant Ormsby, who later retired with the rank of Captain (left) and Lieutenant Thirsten, who was killed during World War II, on the quayside, kitted out for the deployment.

(Simon's Town Museum)

The Mersey Class Minesweeping Trawlers *Eden* (ex *Thomas Johns*) and *Foyle* (ex *John Edmund*) were allocated to the Union of South Africa, together with the Survey Ship **HMS Crozier** to form the nucleus of a South African Naval Service. The three ships left Plymouth, bound for the Cape, on 28 November 1921. They were commissioned as units of the SANS on 1 April 1922 and the names *Eden* and *Foyle* were changed to *Immortelle* and *Sonneblom*. On 31 March 1934, due to cutbacks in defence spending, the two trawlers were paid off and handed back to the Royal Navy, becoming once again *Eden* and *Foyle*. They returned to the UK, manned by personnel taken from *Carlisle* and *Daffodil*. *Eden* remained in reserve until 1942, when she was hulked, eventually being scrapped in 1947. *Foyle* was active throughout World War II and was sold in 1947 for commercial use, fishing and trading until 1954 when she was broken up.

(Simon's Town Museum)

The Modified Leander Class Light Cruiser *Amphion*, 6,908 tons, mounting eight 6" guns, was launched at Portsmouth Dockyard on 26 July 1934. She served at Simon's Town as the Flagship of Vice Admiral Sir Francis L.Tottenham from 1935 to 1938. She was then transferred to the Royal Australian Navy, commissioning as *HMAS Perth* in June 1939, but was sunk by Japanese torpedoes in the Sunda Strait on 1 March 1942.

(Simon's Town Museum)

The Minesweeping Sloop *Milford* which was built under the 1930 Estimates and launched at Devonport Dockyard on 11 June 1932, served on the Africa Station during the 1930s. During the early years of World War II she was based at Freetown. She sank the Vichy French submarine *Poncelet* on 8 November 1940. In 1943 she was found to be unfit for further operational service and was laid up at Ardrossan. During 1944 she was refitted on Teesside, and served as a submarine escort and target with the 10th and 7th Submarine Flotillas until after the end of the War. She was transferred from the Reserve Fleet to the British Iron & Steel Corporation on 3 June 1949 and was allocated to T.W. Ward, for demolition at Hayle. (Simon's Town Museum)

The Sloop *Rochester*, which was one of a group built in the Royal Dockyards during the Depression, was launched at Chatham on 16 July 1931 and served at the Cape in the mid-1930's. During World War II she was involved with the sinking of four U-Boats; *U-204* (with *Mallow* in 1941), *U-82* (with *Tamarisk* in 1942), *U-213* (with *Erne* and *Sandwich* in 1942) and *U-135* (with *Mignonette* and *Balsam* in 1943). After the War *Rochester* was disarmed and attached to the Navigation School at **HMS Dryad** as a training ship. She was sold to Clayton & Davie for demolition on 6 January 1951.

(Simon's Town Museum)

HMS Weston: This ship was another of the Deptford type Sloops built in the Royal Dockyards during the "Hungry Thirties." She was laid down at Devonport as **Weston Super Mare** but, according to legend, was generally referred to as "**Aggie on Horseback**," which was considered to be disrespectful to Dame Agnes Weston, the famed patron of the Royal Sailors' Rests. The ship was renamed and launched as **Weston** on 27 July 1932. She survived World War II and was broken up at Gelleswick Bay in 1947.

(Simon's Town Museum)

Fish for tea: Although large shoals of fish are still seen in False Bay, stocks have been severely depleted since the nineteen sixties. Before that it was usual to find many thousands of fish trapped whenever the graving dock was pumped dry. This photograph shows one of the Shoreham Class sloops on the blocks with a couple of tons of fish on the floor of the dock destined for the tables of the Dockyard workers and other townsfolk.

(Simon's Town Museum)

On 5 April 1937 **Amphion** was in Table Bay, dressed overall, to welcome the new Governor General, Sir Patrick Duncan, who was arriving on board the ***Union Castle*** Mailship.

(Simon's Town Museum)

The Light Cruiser **Neptune** was completed at HM Dockyard Portsmouth in 1933 and served with the Home Fleet until September 1937 when she was transferred to the South Atlantic, arriving at Simon's Town at the end of the year. In 1939 she became the flagship of Vice Admiral d'Oyly Lyon, C-in-C South Atlantic but went to join the Mediterranean Fleet in 1940. *Neptune* fell victim to an Italian minefield off Tripoli on 19 December 1941 and sank. There was only one survivor of her ship's company of around seven hundred men - eighteen of whom were South Africans.

(Simon's Town Museum)

Supermarine Walrus L2262 outside the seaplane hangar in the West Dockyard in 1938. L 2262 was one of 168 Walrus aircraft (ordered under Contract S34422/36 to Specification 37/36 and first flew on 28 June 1938. It was allocated to No 3 Aircraft Storage Unit for delivery to RAF Simon's Town, arriving towards the end of the year, when this photograph was taken. In December 1939 it was transferred to No 711 (Catapult) Squadron, which was absorbed into No 700 Squadron on 21 January 1940. It was allocated to the cruiser *Sussex* to replace her Osprey aircraft. In August 1940 L 2262 was transferred to *Devonshire* Flight of No 700 Squadron and on 14 May 1941 was "written off". (Simon's Town Museum)

The light cruiser **Neptune** visited East London in 1939, just before the outbreak of World War II. In this picture, showing the ship berthed in the Buffalo River, her Hawker Osprey K8575, can be seen mounted on the catapult.

(Simon's Town Museum)

A Great Dane named "*Just Nuisance*" was well known to RN matelots visiting Simon's Town between 1940 and 1944. He frequented the Africa Station Club in Simon's Town and the Union Jack Club in Cape Town, where he is pictured with some friends, including a rating from *Carnarvon Castle*. To get from one club to the other he used the train and according to popular legend, would guide matelots who had imbibed too freely in Cape Town to the station and make sure that they caught the right train to Simon's Town. "*Nuisance*" died on 1 April 1944 and was buried with full military honours at the Signal Station on top of Red Hill.

(Simon's Town Museum)

The Cunard Line Troopships **Queen Mary** and **Aquitania** paid brief visits to Simon's Bay during the early years of World War II. This photograph was taken during the period 28 to 31 May 1940.

(Simon's Town Museum)

While the members of the First Australian Expeditionary Force were honing their unarmed combat skills on the fixtures, fittings and populace of the City of Cape Town, a strong North Westerly gale blew up and the tenders which were to return them to their troopships out in Table Bay were unable to put to sea. In order to avoid delays, the troopships sailed for Simon's Town and trains were arranged to convey approximately 20,000 troops on the twenty two mile journey, noted for its twenty two railway stations, between the "Mother City" and "Snoekie." This photograph, taken from an Avro Anson maritime patrol aircraft of 32 Squadron, shows the Cunarders **Queen Mary** and **Aquitania**, being escorted out of Simon's Bay on 31 July 1940 by the Cruiser **HMAS Australia**. All three ships shown were built by John Brown & Co. Ltd. at Clydebank, **HMAS Australia** having been launched on 17 March 1927, and all three survived the War. The Cruiser was sold to T.W. Ward in July 1955 and broken up at Barrow-in-Furness.

(M.J. Mitchell)

HMS Albatross: This Seaplane Carrier was launched at Cockatoo Island Dockyard, Sydney, on 23 January 1928 and was completed for service with the Royal Australian Navy on 26 April 1933. She was designed to carry nine Supermarine Seagull III amphibians but never embarked more than six of these aircraft. In March 1933 she paid off into reserve but in 1938 was handed over to the Royal Navy in part payment for the light cruiser *Apollo,* which eventually became **HMAS Hobart.** During World War II *Albatross* served in various theatres as an aircraft repair ship and base ship. She arrived at Simon's Town on 23 June 1941 for a refit, during which her pole mainmast was removed and replaced by a tripod; paravane gear was installed and shelters for the pom-pom guns' crews were fitted. She sailed from Simon's Town to rejoin the war at sea on 17 August 1941. On 14 August 1944 she was damaged by a long range torpedo while operating in the Seine Bay as a repair ship in support of the Normandy Landings. *Albatross* was paid off in 1945 and sold in 1947. She was later converted to carry immigrants and sailed under the Greek flag as **Hellenic Prince** until being sold for breaking up in 1953.

(SA Naval Museum)

HMS Hermes, the Royal Navy's first purpose-built aircraft carrier, was launched by Armstrongs, on the River Tyne, on 11 September 1919. She arrived in Simon's Bay on 17 August 1944 for structural repairs following a collision with the Armed Merchant Cruiser *Corfu* off Dakar, West Africa. *Hermes* went into drydock on arrival at Simon's Town on 17 August 1941 and remained on the blocks until 2 November. The task of rebuilding the fore end of the ship stretched the resources of the small dockyard but the men rose gallantly to the occasion. The work was supervised by the resident Naval Constructor, Mr H.T. Bentley RCNC.

(Simon's Town Museum)

While *Hermes* was undergoing extensive structural repairs the opportunity was taken to carry out a normal refit. She was fitted with a paravane clump and chains as a protection against moored mines, ready use lockers for additional pom-pom ammunition and a Type 72 RDF radar set, requiring the addition of a twelve inch diameter pole mast, twenty feet long. Due to the changes carried out on board during the refit an inclining experiment, to determine the new position of the ship's centre of gravity, was carried out on 24 January 1942 with the ship afloat in the drydock. Two hundred and sixteen tons of permanent ballast were added as a result of the calculations carried out.

(Simon's Town Museum)

HMS Hermes returned to the War early in 1942 after her protracted stay in Simon's Town. Whilst in drydock her galley was used to provide meals for Commonwealth troops passing through the Dockyard to join troopships out in Simon's Bay. As it happened, the Dockyard's efforts were to no avail as *HMS Hermes* was overwhelmed and sunk by a massive Japanese air attack off Ceylon (Sri Lanka) on 9 April 1942.

(Simon's Town Museum)

Local tugs were used as tenders to convey personnel and stores to and from troopships anchored off Simon's Town during World War II. The S.A. Railways and Harbours tug *Ludwig Weiner*, which was stationed at Simon's Town as the Guardship **HMS *Afrikander*** during World War I, was sent to Simon's Town in 1940 to ferry troops from the Dockyard to the Royal Mail Line Troopship *Andes*, taking over three hundred men per trip. The Naval Tug *St Dogmael* attended **RMS *Queen Elizabeth***, which carried 15000 troops per transatlantic trip in the build up to D-Day, when she visited Simon's Bay as the single ship Convoy WS 19Y in July 1942. Such convoys, comprising one large, fast troopship, often unescorted during ocean passages, were known as "Monster Convoys."

(Simon's Town Museum)

HM Submarine P552: This submarine, built at Quincy (USA), in 1919 as **S1** for the United States Navy, was one of a group transferred to the Royal Navy in 1942. She is seen here at Simon's Town, where she was refitted during the War, leaving her badge painted on the wall of the graving dock as a memento of the visit. **P552** entered the graving dock on 2 June 1943 together with **P614**, which had been launched at Barrow in Furness on 19 October 1940 as the Turkish **Burak Reis**, before being requisitioned in 1942. The old Cooking Lighter was docked at the same time to be cut up for scrap. In 1945 **P552** was laid up at Mombasa, before she was towed to Durban to be broken up, her hull being dismantled in the Prince Edward graving dock.   (Simon's Town Museum)

Judging by the camouflage pattern and recorded ship movements in the cape area it is deduced that the ship in the photograph is **Newcastle** and that the photograph was taken in August 1943. After escorting Convoy WS (Winston's Special) 29 the cruiser drydocked at Simon's Town from 28 August to 11 September 1943. (SA Naval Museum)

The destroyer *Paladin*, launched on 11 June 1941 at Clydebank, saw a considerable amount of action in the Mediterranean, where she depthcharged and sank *U-205* on 17 February 1943, and in the Indian Ocean where she and her sister *Petard* sank the Japanese submarine *I-27* on 12 February 1944. Following this action she retired to Simon's Town for repairs which required drydocking. She entered the graving dock on 27 March and left on 2 May 1944, after shell plating had been replaced and the starboard shaft bracket repaired. She entered the wet dock on 22 July for a tilt test and alignment of torpedo tubes. After the War *Paladin* and *Petard* were converted to Type 16 (limited conversion) Anti-submarine Frigates and during the late 1950s, in deference to a popular television series, *Paladin* adopted the unofficial motto "Have gun; will travel." She arrived at the shipbreakers' yard at Dunston, on the River Tyne, on 25 October 1962.

(SA Naval Museum)

The Southampton class cruiser **Newcastle**, launched at Wallsend on 23 January 1936 by Vickers Armstrongs Ltd., was originally to have been named **Minotaur** but was renamed before completion. At the beginning of 1944 she was part of the 4th Cruiser Squadron, British Eastern Fleet, which she had joined at Kilindini (Kenya) in 1943. Between the raid on Surabaya in May 1944 and the attack on Pankalau Branadan (Dutch East Indies) in November, the ship visited Simon's Town for a DED (Docking and Essential Defects) period. She entered the graving dock on 24 July and was refloated on 25 August. On 17 September she went back into the wet dock for a Tilt Test, to align her gun mountings with the fire control system. **Newcastle** was modernised during 1950 and took part in the Korean War. She was eventually sold for scrap in 1959, arriving at Faslane on 19 August.

(SA Naval Museum)

The Battleship *Howe* called at Cape Town on her way back to the United Kingdom from the Far East, following the surrender of Japan. She was laid down as *Beatty* but was renamed two months before being launched by the Fairfield Shipbuilding & Engineering Co. Ltd. at Govan on 9 April 1940. On her return from war service, *Howe* was laid up at Plymouth and broken up by T.W. Ward at Inverkiething in 1958.

(Simon's Town Museum)

The Battleship *Howe* at Cape Town.   Divisions were held on the Quarterdeck on 16 September 1945.

(SA Naval Museum)

The Hunt Type II destroyer **Wilton** was launched by Yarrows at Scotstoun on 17 October 1941. On 21 September 1945 she entered the graving dock at Simon's Town together with her sister **Lamerton** for a routine docking which lasted until 9 November. On 11 January 1946 she was placed in the wet dock for a Tilt Test, to align the guns with the director, and Breakage readings, to measure hull deflections. The dock was then pumped out and the blocks were prepared to take the aircraft carrier **Colossus**. The photograph shows the ship embarking ammunition from the lighter **Y.C.431** prior to undergoing the Tilt Test. **Wilton** was placed in reserve on her return to the UK and arrived at Faslane on 30 November 1959 to be broken up. (SA Naval Museum)

In 1945 it was decided to relieve the ships' companies of the River Class frigates *Teviot* and *Swale* with SANF personnel while keeping the ships under RN control. The two ships were sent to Cape Town so that the changeover could take place. *Teviot*, built by Hall Russell & Co. Ltd. at Aberdeen, recommissioned in Table Bay Docks on 10 July 1945 and sailed for the Indian Ocean where she was to patrol part of the sea area over which allied aircraft were flying between Colombo and Rangoon. During July 1945 the ship hit an uncharted reef and had to put into Rangoon for repairs. She arrived in Durban on 21 December 1945 and paid off, being kept on a "Care and Maintenance" basis until she sailed for England on 13 September 1946. *Teviot* was in Reserve at Harwich from 1947 to 1952, when she was transferred to Barrow-in-Furness. In 1955 she was towed to Briton Ferry, where she was broken up by T.W. Ward Ltd.

(Simon's Town Museum)

As the light fleet carrier **HMS Colossus** arrived in Table Bay from the Far East on 17 January 1946 her two squadrons, 827 NAS (comprising 12 Fairey Barracudas) and 1836 NAS (comprising 13 Chance Vought Corsairs), took off for RNAS WINGFIELD at Goodwood. Later that month she sailed for Simon's Town, entering the Selbourne Graving Dock on the thirtieth for a Docking and Essential Defects (DED) period. Whilst in drydock bow damage, believed to have been sustained in a collision with a hospital ship in the Indian Ocean, was repaired. The ship undocked on 26 March.   (Colin Belshaw)

Aircraft carriers were seldom seen in Simon's Town and ***Colossus***, by virtue of her size and the fact that she filled the graving dock and towered over the adjoining quays and workshop, attracted a great deal of interest.

(Colin Belshaw)

When *Colossus* arrived in Table Bay on 8 April 1946, following her DED at Simon's Town the Corsairs of 1846 NAS landed on. Unfortunately one aircraft, No. 111, veered to port on "finals" and landed in the Bay. Fortunately, the frigate **HMSAS Transvaal** (ex -*Loch Ard*) was on hand to rescue the pilot. During her second visit to Cape Town the ship embarked 30 new Grumman Hellcats, which can be seen at the forward end of the flight deck in the photograph. These aircraft were dumped overboard off the Southern Cape Coast while the ship was on passage to India. In August 1946 *Colossus* was loaned to the French Navy for an initial period of five years, being purchased by them in 1951. She served as **FNS Arromanches** until the 1970s.(Tom Cutting)

HMS *Indefatigable*: The third ship of the name, a 26,000 ton Fleet Carrier built by John Brown at Clydebank, called at Cape Town in February 1946 to collect surplus naval aircraft and return them to the USA. **RNAS *Wingfield*** prepared thirty brand new Grumman Hellcats and twenty new Piper Cubs to withstand the effects of salt spray during their transatlantic journey and on 19 and 20 February, delivered them to the ship, together with a number of crated Pratt & Whitney engines. Two days out from Cape Town, following a directive from "higher authority", the Captain gave the order for the whole consignment to be dumped overboard. *Indefatigable* had a short but eventful career, being involved in the attack on the battleship ***Tirpitz*** in Kaafjord on 17 July 1944, less than three months after her completion date. On 27 August 1945, as flagship of Task Group 38.5, which was part of Admiral Halsey's Third Fleet, she sailed into Sagami Bay to await the Japanese surrender. The ship was sold for scrap when only twelve years old and arrived at Dalmuir Basin, just down river from her birthplace, on 4 November 1956.

(Crown Copyright)

The photograph, taken in April 1947, shows the Flagship, *Nigeria*, alongside the East Wall with the Sloops *Modeste*, and *Nereide* astern. Alongside the West Wall is *Norfolk*, the last of the three-funnelled "County" Class Cruisers to visit Simon's Town. Hamoaze Court and Solent Court, the two blocks of flats built in 1943 to accommodate naval ratings and "Home Agreement" Dockyard men and their families, can be seen on the hill just above the graving dock. Higher up, the quarries from which stone was taken to construct the Dockyard between 1900 and 1910 still scar the mountainside.

(Simon's Town Museum)

The photograph, taken in the Selbourne Graving Dock at Simon's Town, shows the port propellers of the Flagship *Nigeria*. Each of the four propellers was driven by a Parsons steam turbine developing 18,000 shaft horsepower to give the ship a speed of 31.5 knots at full power. One of the many ships crests painted on the dock wall can be seen (top right).   (SA Naval Museum)

During the Royal Visit in 1947, the Loch Class frigate **HMSAS Transvaal** was pressed into service as a temporary Royal Yacht for the opening of the Princess Elizabeth graving dock at East London. The photograph shows her, with HRH Princess Elizabeth on board, slicing through the ribbon to open the dock.

Simon's Town Museum)

HMS Vanguard, the last battleship to be built for the Royal Navy, dropped anchor in Simon's Bay during the Royal Visit to Simon's Town in 1947 and is seen here with the Admiralty Salvage Tug *St Dogmael* alongside. The peaks above Fish Hoek and Muizenberg can be seen in the background.

(Simon's Town Museum)

The battleship **Vanguard** was a prominent feature of Table Bay Docks during the Royal Visit in 1947. The berths were more accessible than they are today and the ship attracted many sight-seers, particularly at night when she was illuminated. The ship was due to arrive at a time of year when prolonged South Easterly gales are common so arrangements were made for the steam tug **T.S. McEwen** to act as a tender to ferry the Royal Family and local dignitaries to and from the ship if she was forced to anchor out in Table Bay. Fortunately, the weather was calm when she arrived and she was able to occupy the berth allocated.

(Author's Collection)

In 1942 the **SATS General Botha** was taken over as an accommodation ship and store and given back her old name, **Thames**. She was berthed in the basin, had accommodation for 250 men and carried stores and spare gear for submarines, motor launches and trawlers, in addition to fifteen tons of naval stores and provisions. The photograph shows her out in the Bay with the Flagship **Nigeria**, which arrived on station in April 1946, in the background.

(SA Naval Museum)

The men from the **SATS** *General Botha* moved ashore during 1942 to a camp on the plateau above Redhill, freeing the former Cruiser *Thames* for use as a depot ship. After the War she was found to be surplus to requirements and in poor condition and on 13 May 1947 she was towed out into False Bay and sunk by gunfire from Scala Battery.

(Simon's Town Museum)

HM Ships Actaeon and **Nereide** were "chummy ships" on the Station in the years following World War II. The seventh **Actaeon**, named after a hunter in Greek Mythology who was transformed into a stag and killed by his own hounds, was launched by J. I. Thornycroft, at Southampton, on 25 July 1945. She was transferred to the Federal German Navy in 1958 and renamed **SMS Hipper**.

(Simon's Town Museum)

The Later Battle class Fleet Destroyer *Corunna* is shown passing *Theseus* at high speed during exercises off the Cape Peninsula. It was the custom to invite Parliamentarians and the Press to join the Fleet for a "Sea Day" and to witness such serials as gun firing and light jackstay transfers. The photograph shows a day of calm seas and clear skies, typical of such "Sea Days," which prompted M.P.s to ask when disembarking "Do you chaps actually get paid for doing this?" *Corunna*, launched by Swan Hunter on 29 May 1945, was converted to a Fleet Radar Picket during the early 1960s and was later scrapped at Sunderland in 1974.

(The Cape Times)

The salvage tug **St Dogmael** was completed by the Taikoo Dockyard Co. Ltd at Hong Kong in 1918 and spent nearly all her working life at Simon's Town. While on station at the Cape she was used as a target tug and torpedo recovery vessel. In the latter role she could carry ten eighteen inch torpedoes weighing 1500 lbs each. During World War II she served as a tender to visiting troopships such as **Queen Mary**, **Queen Elizabeth** and **Aquitania**. In June 1947 **HMT Briton** (ex-**Bandit**) arrived on station to replace **St Dogmael** and she was laid up pending disposal. This photograph was taken in June 1949, shortly before she was sunk as a target by the flagship **Nigeria**. (SA Naval Museum)

The Salvage and Target Towing Tug *St Dogmael* was replaced by **HMT Briton**, which arrived on Station on 13 June 1947, the year in which she was renamed. She was transferred to Base Disposals Officer, Plymouth, in October 1956 and was sold to Jos de Smedt, of Antwerp, on 20 April 1960. The photograph was taken on 7 March 1950, on her return from a deployment to Mombasa.

(Simon's Town Museum)

HMS Campania was laid down at Belfast on 12 August 1941 as a 17 knot refrigerated cargo ship for Shaw Savill & Albion Co. Ltd and, had she been completed as intended, would have been similar to the 12,000 ton motor vessels *Wairangi* and *Waiwera*. Instead, she was re-designed and was completed on 7 March 1944 as an Escort Aircraft Carrier capable of operating twenty aircraft. During 1944 and 1945 she was employed escorting convoys to and from Northern Russia and her Swordfish aircraft accounted for *U-921* and *U-365*, which had just torpe-doed and severely damaged the destroyer *Cassandra*. In 1951 she was used as a floating exhibition hall and visited ports around the British Isles during the Festival of Britain. On completion of that task she was selected to support the "A - Bomb" trials at Monte Bello, in the Pacific, and sailed from Portsmouth on 10 June 1952, carrying personnel, stores and equipment for the trials. At the beginning of July she arrived at the Cape and spent a few days in Simon's Town before heading for Australia. The trial was held on 3 October and the ship arrived back in Portsmouth to pay off on 15 December, just in time for Christmas leave. She then became a prominent feature of Sheerness Harbour until she was sold for breaking up at Blyth in November 1955. The photo-graph shows what appears to be a Westland Sikorsky S51 "Dragonfly" helicopter on deck. If so, this would probably be the first helicopter to be seen in Simon's Town. (Simon's Town Museum)

HM *Ships Actaeon* and ***Nereide*** are still the largest warships to have visited the Lagoon Port of Knysna which is entered through a narrow gap dominated by the North and South "Heads," between which is a bar which has claimed several ships during the last couple of centuries. For many years the Benn family, descendants of a Plymouth Shipwright, have piloted ships safely across the bar and along the narrow channel to the town jetty.

(Knysna Museum)

The Dido Class Cruiser *Euryalus*, launched on 6 June 1939, was the last Cruiser to be built at Chatham Dockyard and was arguably one of the best looking cruisers ever built for the Royal Navy. She saw a great deal of action during World War II, collecting battle honours in the Mediterranean before being transferred to the North Sea operational area in 1944. She then joined the British Pacific Fleet in January 1945. Her ten sisters were all completed between 1940 and 1942 and the class were involved in many battles in various theatres. Four were lost and one was scrapped as a result of action damage. *Euryalus* was the Flagship at the Cape in the early 1950s, being placed in reserve on her return to the United Kingdom. She arrived at the breakers' yard at Blyth on 18 July 1959, the day before the submarine *Oberon* was launched into the River Medway from the slipway next to the one from which she had set off twenty years before.

(Seven Seas Club)

HMS Nereide docked at Simon's Town in August 1953 before sailing for the Falkland Islands to spend six months as Antarctic Guardship. This was necessary as ships based in the Caribbean, which normally covered the area, had been redeployed to patrol the flightpath of the aircraft carrying HM Queen Elizabeth II on the Transatlantic leg of the Royal Tour. On the West wall are two "W" class Destroyers, the outer one of which has been disarmed, and the Flagship ***Euryalus***.

(Lt Cdr Ivor Howcroft RNR (Rtd))

The Frigate **Loch Ard** was launched by Harland & Wolff at Govan on 2 August 1944 but was completed in May 1945 as **HMSAS Transvaal**. She is shown here leaving the South African Naval Base at Salisbury Island, Durban, to take part in joint RN/SANF exercises. *Transvaal* was scuttled near Smitswinkel Bay, South of Simon's Town, on 3 August 1978.

(Simon's Town Museum)

During the nineteen fifties, ships of the Royal Navy, based at Simon's Town, exercised with ships of the South African Naval Force, based at Durban. The light cruiser *Euryalus* is shown here alongside the main quay at the South African Naval Base at Salisbury Island.
(R Adm (JG) A.S. Davis Collection, SA Naval Museum)

The "W" Class flotilla leader *Kempenfeldt* was completed by John Brown & Co.Ltd. at Clydebank in October 1943. In January 1944 she took part in the Anzio landings and on "D-Day" was part of the force providing support for the landings at Juno Beach. In August she was part of the force which attacked the German Battleship *Tirpitz* in Kaafjord and by November had been transferred to the Far East. At Trincomalee she joined a group which included her sisters *Wrangler*, *Whelp* and *Wessex* to attack oil installations at Pangkalan Brandan. On 28 September 1947, after a period in reserve in the United Kingdom, *Wessex*, *Whelp*, *Wager* and *Kempenfeldt* sailed for Simon's Town where they were laid up alongside the Eastern Wall of the Dockyard as the South Atlantic Reserve Fleet. The first two ships were handed over to the South African Navy to become *Jan van Riebeeck* and *Simon van der Stel* respectively, while *Kempenfeldt* left for England in March 1954, towed by *HMT Warden*. Two years later she was sold to Yugoslavia, where she was refitted and commissioned as *Kotor* - serving in the Yugoslav Navy until 1971. *Wager* left in 1955, joining the Yugoslav Navy as *Pula*.

(Ian D.C. Roberts)

In the years following World War II the ships of the S.A. Naval Force worked very closely with RN vessels based at the Cape. This photograph, showing just how closely they worked on occasions! This photo was taken a few seconds before the stem of *SAS Simon van der Stel* made contact with the starboard quarter of *Pelican*. The Sloop *Pelican*, launched by J.I.Thornycroft Ltd. at Woolston on 12 September 1938, was sold to T.W. Ward Ltd and arrived at Preston on 29 November 1958 to be broken up.

(R Adm (JG) A.S. Davis Collection, SA Naval Museum)

This photograph showing the Light Cruiser *Superb* entering the basin in 1957 illustrates one of the peculiar features of the Simon's Town Yard. In one of the "Home Dockyards" the ship would have been attended by Empire and TID class tugs. Simon's Town, on the other hand, was designed to berth a Cruiser and a couple of Sloops without the assistance of tugs. A ship arriving at Simon's Town would enter the basin and take on board lines from the steam launches. If necessary an anchor would be dropped. Hawsers were then hauled on board and secured to bollards fore and aft and the ship would be moved to the allocated berth by means of a system of capstans and sheaves. Ships moving into the graving dock would be hauled clear of the West Wall to line up with the centreline of the dock and would then be pulled in using capstans at the head of the dock. As the number of berths occupied increased over the years it became impracticable to use this system and the South African Navy now (2000) uses three berthing tugs and two diesel launches. *Superb* was completed in July 1945 and sold for scrap in 1960.   (Reg Biggs)

On 1 April 1957 Mr Selwyn Lloyd, representing Her Britannic Majesty's Government, handed over the Naval Base and Dockyard at Simon's Town to the Government of the Union of South Africa. Continued co-operation between the two navies was ensured by the signing of the Simon's Town Agreement, which remained in force until the 1980s. The South African Navy had moved its main base from Salisbury Island, in Durban, in advance of the Hand-over. The photograph shows Mr Selwyn Lloyd presenting William Croome with the last Imperial Service Medal to be awarded in the Dockyard, with the Cruiser *Ceylon* in the background.

(Simon's Town Museum)

Simon's Town pubs proudly displayed mementoes of visiting ships. The bar in the St George Hotel had a board displaying badges and names of visiting RN ships side by side with those of the South African Navy, which took over the Simon's Town Base on 1 April 1957. If the "Jimmy" of *Sparrow* is still wondering what happened to his Sunday Ensign, a quiet word with Bombs O'Neill, Yorky Irving, Taff Thomas, Taff Williams and Pincher Martin at the next reunion dinner might prove to be enlightening. (Simon's Town Museum)

Vice Admiral Sir Geoffrey Robson, who is seen being rowed ashore in Table Bay by the officers of the Frigate **Burghead Bay**, served as C-in-C from 1956 until 1958 when he handed over to Vice Admiral Sir Dymock Watson. One of the Type 41 "Big Cats," (possibly **Puma**), can be seen on the other side of **Burghead Bay**, which was transferred to Portugal in 1959 to become **Alvares Cabral**. She was later to re-visit Simon's Town in November 1969.

(SA Naval Museum)

Helicopters are a common sight at Simon's Town these days but in 1958, when the Ice Patrol Ship *Protector* called, they were a rarity. The ship's red Westland Sikorsky S 55 Whirlwind, XA 866, which landed at Cole Point on 17 April 1958 was the first such aircraft that most of the inhabitants had seen at close quarters and attracted quite a crowd.   (Simon's Town Museum)

On 29 March 1950 the destroyer *Wessex* commissioned as **HMSAS Jan Van Riebeeck**. Originally she was to have been named **Zenith** but was launched from the Fairfield Yard at Govan on 2 September 1943 as *Wessex*. Following the Japanese surrender *Wessex* assisted with the repatriation of Commonwealth POWs before returning to England, where she was placed in reserve at Devonport. In 1947, she was one of four "W" Class ships allocated to the South Atlantic Reserve Fleet at Simon's Town. She paid off into reserve in 1953 when her sistership **Whelp** commissioned as **HMSAS Simon Van Der Stel**, after which the two destroyers took turn about to be in commission. The photograph shows "*JvR*" alongside the East Wall at Simon's Town during her modernisation and conversion to carry two Westland Wasp A/S helicopters. The "Gooseneck " crane in the background was demolished during the nineteen sixties.

(Simon's Town Museum)

The "Big Cats," propelled by eight Admiralty Standard Range (ASR) 1 diesel engines (giving them a range of 7500 miles at 16 knots) were ideal for patrolling the vast Southern Oceans and visiting the remote islands situated there, using Simon's Town as a base. *Puma*, which was launched by Scotts of Greenock on 30 June 1954, is pictured here off the Bullnose at Simon's Town on 13 February 1960. In 1964 she emerged from a refit with a "mack" mainmast supporting a Type 965 radar antenna and later her anti-aircraft capability was improved when the 40mm Bofors was replaced by a Seacat missile system. She arrived at the breakers' yard at Blyth on 10 December 1976. (Simon's Town Museum)

Exercise Shop Window: During 1961 *Victorious* paid a visit to Cape Town and participated in joint exercises with ships of the South African Navy. This photograph, taken on 18 February 1961, shows *Lynx* and *Blackpool* and the South African Type 15 Frigate *SAS Vrystaat* (ex-*HMS Wrangler*) firing their Anti-Submarine Mortar Mk.10 (Limbo) while escorting *Victorious*.

(Simon's Town Museum)

In 1962 the South African Frigate/Despatch Vessel **SAS Good Hope** (ex-**HMS Loch Boisdale**) sailed from Simon's Town carrying the ashes of Vice Admiral Sir Herbert A.Packer K.C.B, C.B.E, which were to be scattered at sea. Admiral Packer, who was married to the South African born novelist Joy Packer, was the Commander-in-Chief at the Cape from 1950 to 1952, flying his flag in **Bermuda**.

(Simon's Town Museum)

Collisions: During Naval Exercises, with ships operating at close quarters, there is always a fairly high risk of collision. During CAPEX exercises over the years, minor collisions occurred between the Frigate **Diomede** and **RFA Tideflow** and, earlier, between the destroyer **SAS Simon Van der Stel** and the Frigate **Pelican**. A more serious collision occurred during CAPEX 63 when, on 28 July 1963, the Algerine Class Minesweeper **SAS Pietermaritzburg** (ex-**HMS Pelorus**), ploughed into the port bow of **Leopard**, resulting in the death of eighteen year old Able Seaman Thomas Bolton, of Aberdeen, aboard the British ship. The South African Deputy State Attorney found that there was contributary negligence on the part of the Officers of the Watch on both ships.

(SA Naval Museum)

The streamlined "A" Class submarine *Alliance*, seen here in East London Harbour, took part in CAPEX 63 (Cape Exercises), together with the Frigates **HMS Whitby** and **HMS Leopard**. She was completed by Vickers Armstrong Ltd. at Barrow-in-Furness on 14 May 1947 and was modernised and streamlined in the late 1950s. *Alliance* is now (2000) high-and-dry on the hard at Gosport, where she is one of the major attractions at the RN Submarine Museum. (Author's Collection)

In the early nineteen sixties the Fleet Replenishment Tanker **RFA Wave Baron** took part in a CAPEX involving **SA Ships Vrystaat**, **Good Hope**, **Transvaal** and the Royal Navy frigate **Puma**. **HM Submarine Trespasser** and the American submarine **USS Chivo** also took part. The tanker was one of a class of twenty one steam turbine propelled, fifteen knot tankers ordered towards the end of World War II by the Ministry of War Transport. She was launched on 19 February 1946 at Haverton Hill, on the River Tees, as **Empire Flodden**, but was completed as an RFA. All but one of the class became RFA vessels, the exception was purchased by tanker owners John I. Jacobs & Co. Ltd. and completed as **Beechwood**. **Wave Baron** was one of the last three of the class to remain in service. She was broken up at Bilbao in 1972.

(Author's collection)

In July 1965 the Mayor of Simon's Town, Councillor L.J.D.Gay, handed over a granite block commemorating the establishment of the Royal Naval Dockyard in Simon's Town in 1884 to Vice Admiral J.M.D.Gray, C-in-C South Atlantic and South American Station. The block was to be delivered to His Worship the Mayor of Portsmouth to be placed in the local cathedral together with similar blocks from dockyard towns around the World.

(Die Burger)

The Big Cat Class diesel frigate *Jaguar* was completed at Dumbarton on 12 December 1959, the last warship to be built at the yard of William Deny. Soon afterwards she arrived at Chatham Dockyard, where she lay in No.3 Basin while a Board of Inquiry investigated the presence of blasting grit in her main gearing. Whilst alongide she was used by the "Carry On" team to shoot scenes for their film "Watch your stern!" She arrived at Simon's Town on 25 June 1965 to replace *Leopard* on station. She was sold to Bangladesh on 6 July 1978 and renamed **Ali Haider**. She was still in service in 2000.

(Author's Collection)

Even when the Governments of Great Britain and the Republic of South Africa were diametrically opposed on the question of Rhodesian Independence, Royal Naval vessels were frequent visitors to Simon's Town. The Daring Class ship *Dainty* arrived on 23 February 1968 en route from Trinidad to the Mozambique Channel where she was to patrol off Beira to intercept tankers carrying oil which could eventually find its way, via the pipeline, to Ian Smith's Rhodesia. The ship called again on 27 June 1969 on her way home. *Dainty* was one of four Daring Class ships with a 220 volt D.C. electrical system. Four other ships, with Alternating Current systems, proved the superiority of the 440 volts 60 cycles per second (Hertz) system which was adopted for all major warships built subsequently.

(R. Adm (JG) A.G. Soderlund SA Navy)

SANEX 69: The Royal Naval contingent involved in the joint British/South African exercise held during 1969 comprised *Galatea*, *Lincoln* and *Cleopatra* and *HM Submarines Finwhale* and *Ambush* and the Survey Vessels *Beagle* and *Bulldog*. The South African Navy provided the Type 12 Frigate *SAS President Pretorius*, the Helicopter Carrying Destroyer *SAS Simon van der Stel* and the Replenishment Tanker *SAS Tafelberg*. The photograph shows *Finwhale* (inboard) and *Ambush* in the Dockyard after the exercise. In the background is the Frigate *SAS President Kruger* which had recently been modernised and fitted with a helicopter hangar and flight deck and Jupiter search radar. Behind her can be seen the funnel of her sister *SAS President Steyn* which was in Dockyard hands for a similar conversion. The South African ships externally resembled the RN Type 12s but the internal layout was similar to that of *HMNZ Ships Otago* and *Taranaki*.

(SA Naval Museum)

RFA **Hebe** and her sister **Bacchus** were completed in 1962 by Henry Robb & Co. at Leith for the British India Steam Navigation Co. Ltd. and were taken over by MoD(N) on a long term bareboat charter basis. Handier and more economical than the remaining Fort Class they operated between the Home Dockyards and overseas bases carrying a variety of naval stores. They also carried the furniture and effects of naval families to and from the UK in Chacons, small containers designed in Chatham Dockyard for that purpose. The photograph shows **Hebe** alongside the East Wall in November 1969. SA Naval vessels in the basin include ten Coastal Minesweepers, the largest group of Ton Class vessels outside the Royal Navy.   (SA Naval Museum)

Frigates were regular visitors to Simon's Town during the 'sixties and 'seventies. Closure of the Suez Canal forced them, for a time, to use the Cape Route to and from the Far East, the Persian Gulf, and the patrol area off Beira, in the Indian Ocean. This aerial photograph, taken early in the 1970s shows the Yarrows-built Type 12 Frigate **Brighton** outboard of the Devonport-built Tribal **Tartar** at West Wall North. **Tartar** was drydocked from 27 May to 4 June 1970 in Simon's Town. The ship in the foreground is the Boom Defence Vessel **SAS Somerset**, formerly **HMS Barcross**, which is now (2000) attached to the Maritime Museum in Cape Town. Laid up out in the Bay are, from left to right, the Frigate/Despatch Vessel **SAS Good Hope** (ex - **Loch Boisdale**) and the Type 15 Frigate **SAS Vrystaat** (ex - **Wrangler**). (SA Navy)

The sixth *Oberon* was in Simon's Town on 31 July 1970, which is remembered as "Black Tot Day," the day on which the pipe "Up spirits" and the issue of the traditional rum ration was made for the last time aboard R.N. ships. The submarine returned to South Africa during the following year, being placed in the graving dock on 30 October 1971 and taken out on 9 November. The launch of *Oberon* from No. 7 Slip at Chatham Dockyard on Saturday 19 July 1959 by HRH Princess Marina, Duchess of Kent, marked the re-entry of the Yard into the submarine building business. *Oberon* was the first RN submarine to have a casing constructed largely of glass reinforced plastic and had an ignominious start to her career when she grounded just off the Esplanade at Rothesay shortly before 2100 on 12 January 1961, during her sea acceptance trials. She was sold in 1987.

(R. Adm (JG) A.G. Soderlund SA Navy)

The design of **Hecla**, and her sisterships **Hecate** and **Hydra** was based on that of the Royal Research Ship **Discovery**. All three were laid down at Yarrows' own shipyard and their recently acquired Blythswood yard during 1964. In 1969 the South African Navy ordered a similar but slightly faster ship from the same builder, the South African ship having geared diesel propulsion instead of the earlier diesel electric propulsion. This vessel, **SAS Protea**, was the first ship to be laid down on the covered berth at Yarrow (Shipbuilders) Ltd Blythswood facility and was launched on 14 July 1971.

(Author's Collection)

Throughout the 1960s and 1970s, the Royal Navy kept its own Furnace Fuel Oil (FFO) tank in the S.A.Naval tank farm at Seaforth. With the demise of the steam frigate this fuel became surplus to requirements and the final stock was used during the 1980s to bunker the Falklands Conflict veteran *RMS St Helena*, which burned a blend of FFO and marine gas oil in her propulsion and auxiliary diesel engines. The photograph shows the Leander Class Frigate *Danae* leaving Simon's Town after a refuelling stop in the 1970s.   (SA Navy)

The Royal Yacht *Britannia*, flying the flag of the Flag Officer Royal Yachts (FORY) but without any members of the Royal Family onboard, called at Simon's Town during a positioning voyage in 1972. *Britannia* was launched by John Brown & Co. Ltd. at Clydebank on 16 April 1953. The design of the hull and propulsion machinery was based on that of the 21 knot British Railways steamers *Amsterdam* and *Arnhem*, built at the same yard for the Harwich - Hook-of-Holland service in 1950. (Simon's Town Museum)

The hunter-killer submarine *Dreadnought* which called during 1973, was the first nuclear powered vessel to visit Simon's Town. She is seen here arriving at the Bullnose, escorted by *De Neys*, the first Voith-Schneider tug to be built and operated in South Africa, and the diesel launch *DL5*, formerly Admiralty *HL(D) 3939*. In the background can be seen the cable ship *Cable Restorer*, built in 1944 as *HMS Bullfrog*, the Mooring Lighter and the Algerine Class fleet minesweeper *SAS Pietermaritzburg*. *"PMB,"* serving as *HMS Pelorus* with Commander Nelson in command, led one of the columns across the English Channel on D-Day, proudly flying the signal "Nelson in the van." On 3 September 1945, as part of the Sixth Minesweeping Flotilla, she led the Royal Navy back into Singapore after the surrender of Japanese forces on the island.

(SA Naval Museum)

Cape Exercises (CAPEX) involving the Royal Navy and the South African Navy were held regularly in the South Atlantic and Southern Indian Oceans while the Simon's Town Agreement was in force. The photograph, taken on board the "broad beam" Leander Class frigate *Diomede* during a CAPEX in the mid-1970s shows the ship approaching the starboard side of **RFA** *Tideflow* to refuel. Unfortunately the two ships made contact during the evolution resulting in slight damage to both.

(R Adm (JG) A.E. Rudman SA Navy)

RFA Grey Rover was one of three sisters delivered by Swan Hunter in 1969/70. The ships were initially fitted with the Ruston AO "Space frame" diesel engines which proved to be unsuccessful and were replaced. She is shown here leaving Simon's Town during the nineteen eighties in a loaded condition.

(SA Navy)

Visit by **Norfolk** - For political reasons ships of the Royal Navy avoided calling at Simon's Town between 1975, when South African forces invaded the newly independent Republic of Angola, and 1994 when the present South African government took office. The visit by **Norfolk**, which arrived in Simon's Bay on 31 January 1994, restored a link that had been broken nineteen years and ten months earlier with the sailing of the last RN visitor.

(R Adm (JG) A.E. Rudman SA Navy)

The Royal Yacht **Britannia** returned to the Cape in 1995, carrying Her Majesty Queen Elizabeth II, visiting both Cape Town and Simon's Town. The presence of the "Table Cloth" on Table Mountain indicates that a strong South Easterly wind is blowing.

(SA Navy)

Badges in the Selborne Graving Dock: It became traditional, during World War II, for each ship visiting the graving dock in Simon's Town to paint its badge on the dock wall as a memento of the visit. As time went by, the earlier badges began to fade and it was the unwritten rule that a visiting ship would add or freshen up its own badge and freshen up two others. Supervision was not always what it should have been and mistakes were made; for instance, the Armed Merchant Cruiser **Asturias** has somehow become "*Astovas.*" All the badges in the drydock were repainted in 1997 as part of the "Navy 75" celebrations. (SA Navy)

The Type 23 Frigate **Monmouth**, named to commemorate the "Black Duke," passes Mouille Point, with its now-defunct red and white striped lighthouse, on her way into Table Bay to spend Christmas 1997 in Cape Town. During January 1998, while the ship was alongside the Waterfront in Cape Town, the British Defence Evaluation Research Agency (DERA) used her as a floating exhibition of British defence equipment and shipbuilding technology.

(SA Navy)

The Type 22 (Batch 3) frigate *Chatham*, completed by Swan Hunter Shipbuilders at Wallsend in May 1990 became the first of her class to visit a South African port when she arrived at Simon's Town in April 1997. The South African Navy celebrated its 75th Anniversary on 1 April 1997 and ships from thirteen foreign navies arrived to join the celebrations. Among those present were the ex-RN vessels **PNS Babur** (*ex-Amazon*) from Pakistan, **KD Hang Tuah** (*ex-Mermaid*) from Malaysia and **RSS Perseverance** (*ex-RFA Sir Lancelot*) from Singapore.

(Sheila Rice)

As the Twentieth Century drew to a close and with increasing Royal Navy commitments in the South Atlantic and West Africa, the ports of South Africa are once again being visited by Royal navy warships. *Argyll* arrived at Cape Town on 3 October 2000 after a busy period of operations off Sierra Leone.

(Crown Copyright)

Index of Ships' Names